Hot Dog!

Eleanor Roosevelt Throws a Picnic

By Leslie Kimmelman

Illustrated by Victor Juhasz

To Jennifer—friend, colleague, and
fellow history enthusiast
                    —Leslie

For Magnus, Joli, and Milo
                    —Victor

Sleeping Bear Press™

315 E. Eisenhower Parkway, Suite 200
Ann Arbor, MI 48108
www.sleepingbearpress.com

Printed and bound in the United States.

10 9 8 7 6 5 4 3 2 1

Library of Congress Cataloging-in-Publication Data

Kimmelman, Leslie.
Hot dog! : Eleanor Roosevelt throws a picnic / written by Leslie Kimmelman ;
illustrated by Victor Juhasz.
pages cm
Summary: "In June of 1939, British monarchs King George VI and Queen Elizabeth
visit America, the first visit ever by reigning British royalty. As part of the festivities,
First Lady Eleanor Roosevelt hosts an all-American picnic that includes hot dogs, a
menu item that shocks some people"—Provided by publisher.
ISBN 978-1-58536-830-3
1. Roosevelt, Eleanor, 1884-1962—Juvenile literature. 2. Presidents' spouses—United
States—Juvenile literature. 3. Visits of state—United States—Juvenile literature.
4. George VI, King of Great Britain, 1895-1952—Travel—United States—Juvenile
literature. 5. Elizabeth, Queen, consort of George VI, King of Great Britain, 1900-2002
—Travel—United States—Juvenile literature. 6. Royal visitors—Great Britain—
Juvenile literature. 7. Royal visitors—United States—Juvenile literature. I. Juhasz,
Victor, illustrator. II. Title.
E807.1.K56 2014
973.917092—dc23   2013024897

Hot diggity dog!

Eleanor Roosevelt really liked hot dogs. She liked to eat them, and she liked to cook them up on the grill. In her family, she was famous for her hot dog roasts.

But when her husband, Franklin, was elected president of the United States, there wasn't much time for hot dog roasts.

Times were tough in the United States in the 1930s. Many people were without jobs, food, or even a place to live. The president was working hard to make things better. Since he couldn't walk or move about easily, he counted on Eleanor to travel around the country for him.

As a young girl, Eleanor had been very shy. She'd never wanted to be First Lady. But she worked hard, and she got better and better at speaking in public—she'd *always* been good at listening. Soon Eleanor was as popular as the president.

"Here's what people are saying in Ohio," she'd tell Franklin when she returned to the White House. "And these are the problems in Idaho," she'd say. "And don't forget those poor Californians," she'd remind him. Eleanor never seemed to run out of energy.

There were big problems in the rest of the world, too. The leader of Germany, Adolf Hitler, was threatening the countries around him. It looked as if a huge war might be coming. Eleanor hated war, but this one was going to be hard to avoid.

Being First Lady meant your house—the White House—was always full of people. Sometimes important people visited Washington, D.C., and a dinner was held in their honor. The dinners were usually fancy— "and always hot dog-less," complained Eleanor.

Then, in 1939, the king and queen of England announced they were coming. One hundred and fifty years had passed since the United States had won its independence from Great Britain. No British king or queen had ever set foot on American soil since. It was about time.

"Did you know that Queen Elizabeth is a distant cousin of George Washington?" Eleanor asked her husband. "She's practically a member of the American family!

"So to celebrate the first royal visit," Eleanor continued, "we need an all-American picnic." And what is a picnic, Eleanor probably asked herself, without hot dogs?

After the usual fancy dinner at the White House, Eleanor decided, she and Franklin and the king and queen would travel up to Hyde Park, New York, where the Roosevelt family had a big estate. Eleanor and Franklin loved spending time there.

The main house was too big and formal for a picnic. Instead the picnic would be held at Top Cottage, a simple stone house the president owned on top of a nearby hill. From the porch, guests could see the Hudson River weaving through the valley below, the gentle Catskill and Shawangunk Mountains rising into the sky, and beautiful countryside in every direction. There was no prettier place for leaving the cares of the world behind.

Eleanor planned the menu carefully: smoked turkey, baked ham, cranberry jelly, brown bread, baked beans, green salad, and strawberry shortcake made with local strawberries. And, of course, hot dogs.

"Fine," Franklin agreed. "Anything but spinach. I'm the president, and I shouldn't have to eat spinach if I don't want to."

Not everyone was pleased with the menu. Thousands of letters poured into the White House, from New York and Michigan, from South Carolina and Kansas and the other states. All about hot dogs.

"Everyone knows that a hot dog is most indigestible," read one. "For mercy's sake, no hot dogs for Europe to laugh about," begged another. "Must you feed the queen hot dogs?" asked a third. "It is not exactly a lady's fare. And I think we all agree the queen is a lady."

Being First Lady and speaking on the president's behalf had taught Eleanor how to stick up for herself. In her daily newspaper column, she wrote:

Oh dear, oh dear, so many people are worried that "the dignity of our country will be imperiled" by inviting royalty to a picnic, particularly a hot dog picnic.... Let me assure you, dear readers, that ... there will be plenty of other food, and ... the more important guests will be served with due formality.

And so, on June 11, 1939, Eleanor woke up, did her morning sit-ups, and went to church. Then she dashed up to Top Cottage to get things ready for King George, Queen Elizabeth, President Roosevelt, and about two hundred of their closest friends and neighbors.

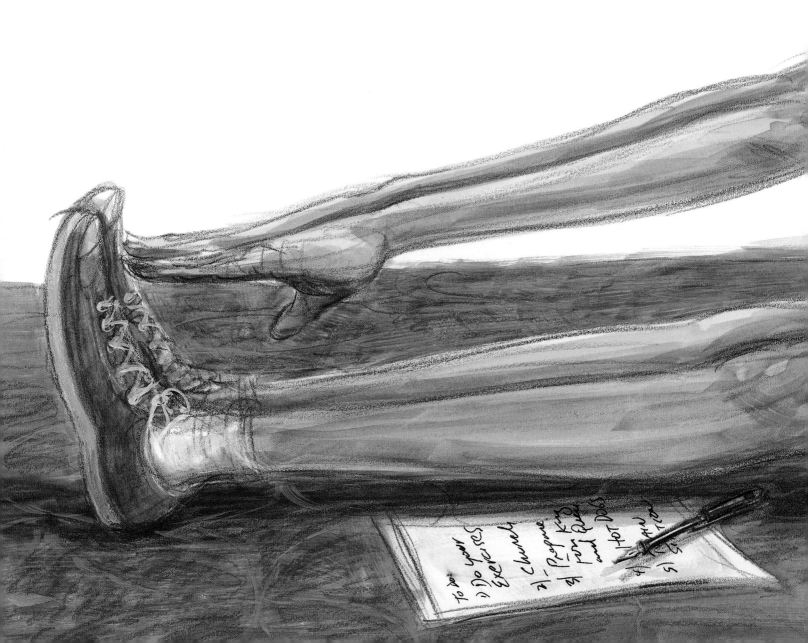

The king and queen pulled up in a car driven by the president himself. "Welcome!" Eleanor greeted them. "How was your ride?"

She could guess the answer. Franklin had a special car that he worked with hand controls. He loved driving it—the faster, the better. As Eleanor suspected, on this sunny afternoon he'd been showing off, racing their majesties up bumpy roads, through the woods, and around steep, twisty turns to the picnic site. What a wild trip!

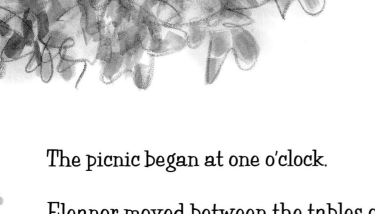

The picnic began at one o'clock.

Eleanor moved between the tables on the porch and those on the lawn, chatting with her guests and tasting everything from turkey fit for a king (and queen!) to berries so juicy they practically exploded with sweetness.

During the feast Native Americans performed traditional dances, music, and folktales. It's safe to say that it was the first time their majesties had ever heard the Navajo Potato song!

Eleanor's famous hot dogs were a first, too—arranged just so on a fancy silver tray. The royal couple had never tried such food. King George picked one up with his fingers and ate it with gusto... and mustard! He even came back for seconds. But the queen was puzzled. She asked, "How do you eat this?"

"Very simple," replied President Roosevelt. "Push it into your mouth and keep pushing it until it is all gone."

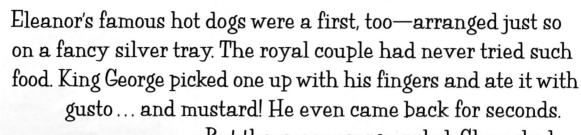

Was that a proper way for a queen to eat?
Of course not! She cut the hot dog into little
pieces and ate it daintily with her fork.

The royal visitors had to leave that evening to begin the long trip back to England. The sun was setting as the townspeople gathered at the train station and up and down the banks of the Hudson River. They sang off King George and Queen Elizabeth with an old Scottish tune: "*Should auld acquaintance be forgot, and never brought to mind . . .*" The warm, gracious king and queen who had visited their little town would not soon be forgotten.

As music filled the air and the train chugged slowly down the tracks,
Eleanor waved to her new friends. Franklin called out one last time:
"Good luck to you! All the luck in the world."

Three months later, German tanks rolled into the country of Poland. World War II had begun. England, and later the United States, would see many years of fighting before peace came again. The Roosevelts and the royal couple were never far from each other's thoughts as their two countries battled side by side against their enemies.

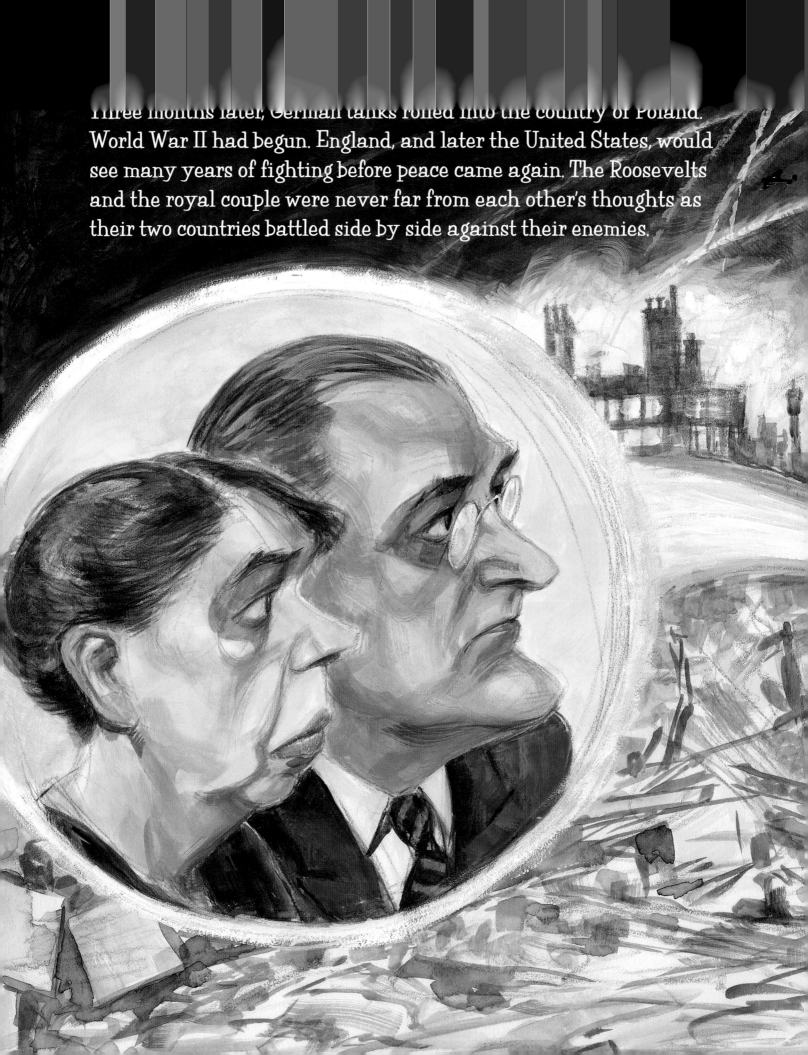

President Roosevelt had promised to visit King George and
Queen Elizabeth at their castle in England. It never happened.
The president died before the war was over. Eleanor would
later take the trip alone.

June 11, 1989, was another perfect picnic day. Fifty years had passed, and an anniversary picnic was being held at Hyde Park. The children who'd been guests at the 1939 picnic were much older now, and some of them returned to eat and share memories. Queen Elizabeth sent a special message: "The memory of the picnic was a source of strength and comfort to the king and me through the dark days of the Second World War, which followed so soon after our visit."

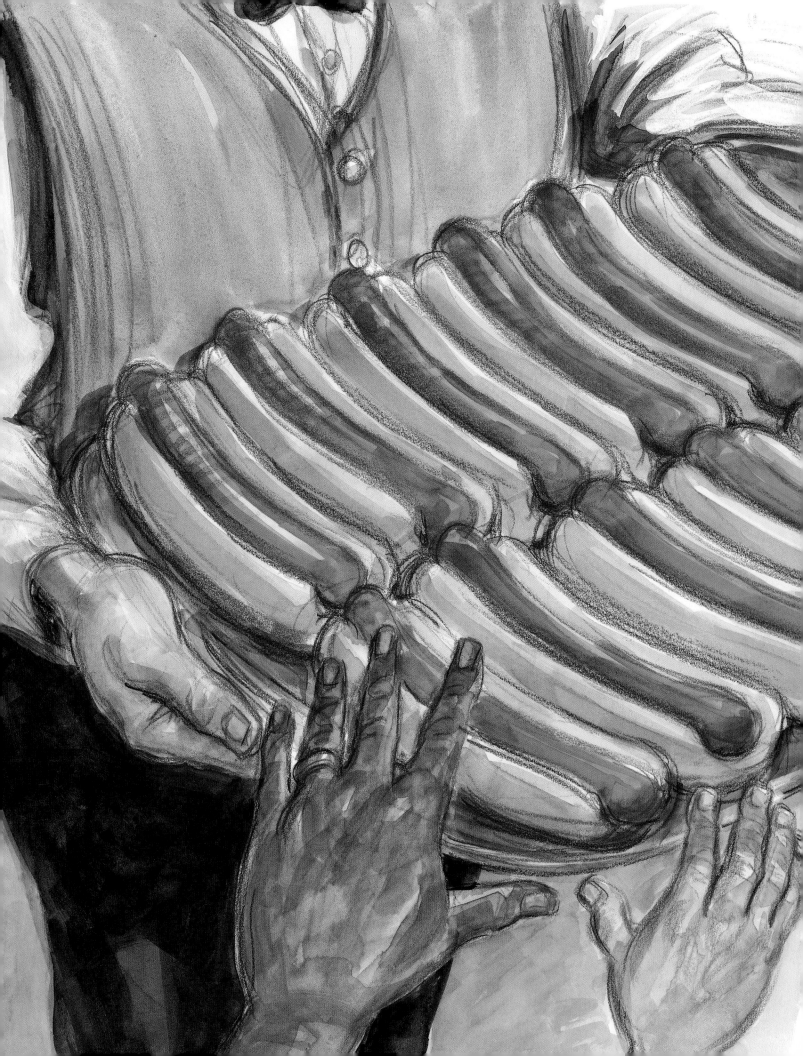

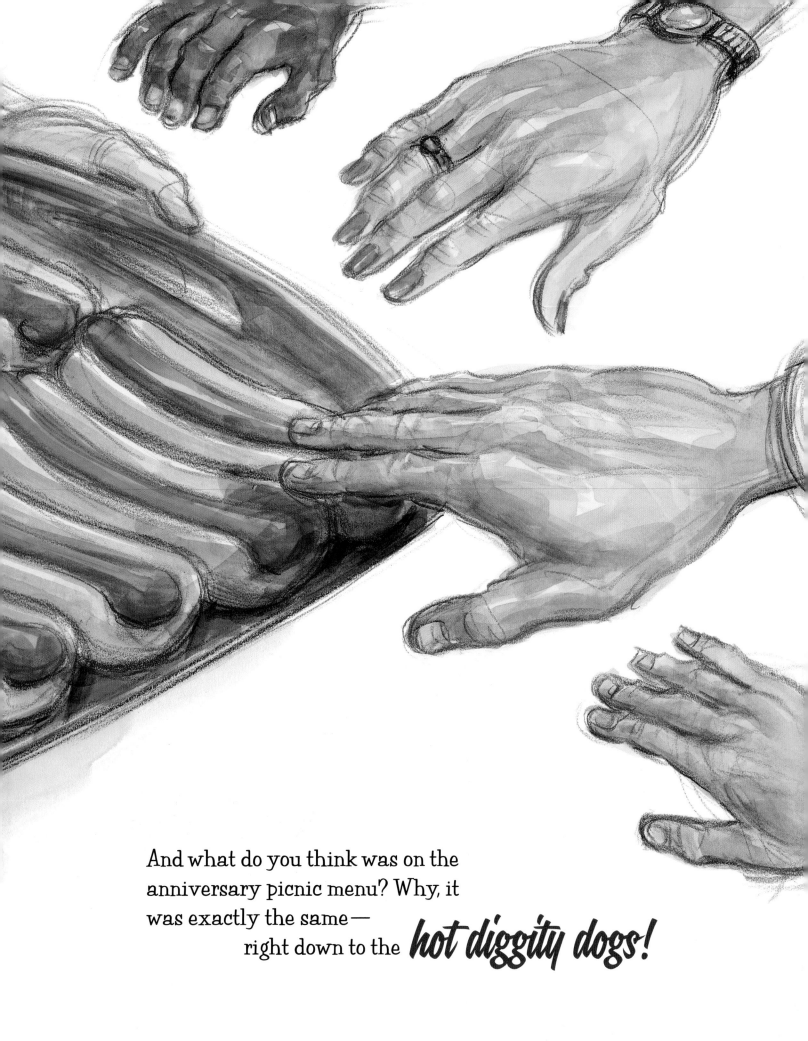

And what do you think was on the
anniversary picnic menu? Why, it
was exactly the same—
           right down to the *hot diggity dogs!*

Author's Note

The 1939 royal visit and the picnic at Hyde Park are true events, though, of course, different people remember details differently. The research library at Hyde Park holds the letters people wrote to Mrs. Roosevelt about her menu. The queen and king reacted to the hot dogs just as written.

Franklin Roosevelt was a remarkable man. He became the thirty-second president of the United States in 1933, during the Great Depression—a time when millions of Americans were out of work and desperately trying to scrape together enough money to live on. He continued as president during World War II, seeing the country most of the way to victory. He died in office shortly before the end of the war.

What made his accomplishments even more extraordinary was that he had been stricken with polio as a young man and was mostly confined to a wheelchair. Roosevelt was the only president to be elected four times in a row; a law was passed later, limiting future presidents to two terms (eight years).

First Lady Eleanor Roosevelt was equally remarkable. Since Franklin couldn't move about easily, she became his traveling eyes and ears. She spoke up passionately for children, for workers, on behalf of women and minorities— for anyone who needed a helping hand—letting people know that their government was listening. After Franklin's death, Eleanor became the first U.S. ambassador to the newly formed United Nations. Her work there earned her the nickname "First Lady of the World."

King George VI and Queen Elizabeth also led their country through some very difficult years, setting a courageous and gracious example for the British people. The friendship that developed between the two couples helped lay the groundwork for the close cooperation of their countries during the long war years and a friendship with the United States that continues to this day.